GOD MEANT IT *for* GOOD

The Alice T. Brown Story

GOD MEANT IT *for* GOOD

The Alice T. Brown Story

Eileen G. Foreman

Printed in the United States of America

Packaged by Pleasant Word, a division of WinePress Publishing, PO Box 428, Enumclaw, WA 98022. The views expressed or implied in this work do not necessarily reflect those of Pleasant Word, a division of WinePress Publishing. Ultimate design, content, and editorial accuracy of this work are the responsibilities of the author.

Scripture references marked KJV are taken from the King James Version of the Bible.

ISBN 1-57921-628-5
Library of Congress Catalog Card Number: 2003102858

Table of Contents

Introduction

"But as for you, ye thought evil against me, but God meant it unto good, to bring to pass, as it is this day, to save much people alive." Genesis 50:20 (KJV)

The events of September 11, 2001, have forever changed our view of suffering, trials, and tragedy. Instantaneously and simultaneously, thousands of us were rendered heartbroken and experienced significant loss. I have a full life that is rich with experiences and riddled with tragedy. My tragedies are not associated with the September 11 terrorist attacks. I don't claim to have a get-happy-quick bag of tricks, but I have gained some intensely valuable insights that have lifted me from the valley of despair to the mountaintop of victory.

I am sharing my experiences of losing loved ones and living with AIDS because I want to give hope and focus to people who are still wrestling with the losses in their lives. Far too many self-help books contain great notions and few tangible tools. I want this book to be real, plain, and very clear because this isn't meant to be a platform for a made-for-TV movie. I believe deeply in the value of this book for anyone who reads it, so I do not inflate or glamorize presenting my story to you.

To many people, "healing" means the absence of symptoms, the absence of pain, remission of cancerous cells, and a clean bill of health from the doctors. I have learned to expand my definition of "healing" because my understanding of how God heals has changed. I now understand that I can be healed spiritually and develop a well-being that is present with me physically, even though my body is experiencing disease.

The deaths of my husband and my son were devastating losses that broke my heart. One of my victories is an awareness that I needed to develop and nurture healing relationships. Through healing relationships I learned that people receive more when they are giving. Once my spirit was healed, I needed to maintain relationships that would nurture my spirit and help me to continue to grow. Developing healing relationships is the key to creating an environment around me that supports healing vs. suffering, victory vs. defeat.

God Meant It for Good is not a Twelve Step, sixty-second, or three-bullet recipe for overcoming grief, pain, and despair. God Meant It for Good is going to move you to examine the choices available to you when tragedy strikes. I only explore the hows in dealing with tragedy; I am not equipped to explain the whys. I share how my relationship with God is at the core of my successfully moving to victorious living; I now appreciate the concept of Genesis 50:22: God meant it for good.

Working through the tragedies in my life has given me a stronger faith and a great assurance that gives fullness to the life I live, as well as a perspective that I want to share. I offer this gift given to me to all people who find themselves isolated in a life experience that is presenting physical and emotional turmoil. I have come to understand how God takes difficulties, afflictions, and tragedies and makes them opportunities for a close relationship between Him and those people chosen to endure these situations.

I offer you an opportunity to see how I learned the keys to victorious living and, as a result, experienced God's healing power by understanding that God meant it for good.

In the Beginning

Then the word of the Lord came unto me, saying, "Before I formed thee in the belly I knew thee; and before thou camest forth out of the womb I sanctified thee. . . ." Jeremiah 1:5–5 (KJV)

I was born on September 30, 1958, in Baltimore, Maryland. My parents had eight children, five boys and three girls. I was number six and the baby girl. We all had the utmost respect for my parents because they were strict and they did not play around. They believed in discipline and rules, and they did not hesitate to enforce them. My mother was the wild one. She would whip our butts with the first thing she laid her hands on. On the other hand, my father was cool. He would get a hold on us first. Then, once we couldn't move, he would tear us up. We couldn't play the two against each other. If we tried, our butts would be beat again. I never heard my parents curse, and I never saw them fight. The worst thing I remember was an argument where my father threw a tea towel at my mother and made her cry. My mother was a drama queen. I knew she wasn't hurt, but her response was enough to make my father back down. I thought they were such a perfect couple that I just couldn't wait to get married and raise a family just like ours.

We were raised in a Holiness church. Services lasted all day on Sundays and almost every night of the week, and my parents made sure we were there. Believe it or not, I really enjoyed it because it was all I knew. The church was like an extended family. We did almost everything together. We traveled to our sister churches on every holiday, except Christmas. On Sundays we were either eating at church or one of the saints' (that's what we called other members) homes. Just like with all families, some trouble was always brewing. Unfortunately, that's where my family fit in.

We were a poor family. Sometimes we didn't know where our next meal was coming from. God always provided, and we never went without. However, growing up poor in our church was hard, because we were treated differently. Only certain children in the church would be chosen to participate in special programs. These children were from families we referred to as "favorite" families. As children we were pained to watch the favorite children being used all the time for special duties, while we were never asked to be a part. We, on the other hand, were always accused of things that were negative. We were picked on for no apparent reason, as if everyone in the church had permission to alienate us and point at us for anything that went wrong. Even worse, the church deacons and officials were just as bad as some of the members.

I remember when one of my girlfriends and I were standing outside of the restroom and some other kids were playing around. We weren't doing anything, but when we saw one of the deacons headed in our direction, we warned the kids he was coming. The deacon started yelling at me. He ignored the kids playing and let my girlfriend walk away. As I explained to him that I had done nothing and started to walk away, he proceeded to put his hands on me and pulled me back. By this time everyone was watching as I tried to pull away from this man, and they told me to stop what I was doing. Another time, a deacon stopped service and pointed at me. He said I should be removed because I was talking while the preacher was preaching. I had not opened my mouth, but once again I was singled out for doing something wrong. My brothers were treated the same way; we all felt so abused. I lost respect for my church's leadership. By the time I was eighteen, I had enough and decided to leave the church.

My decision to leave the church was connected to my decision to leave home. The two were so intermingled; doing just one would have been too difficult. I was being rebellious and full of myself. I thought I had all the answers, and I did not want to listen to anyone or adhere to any rules in my parents' home.

Off on my own, I was working in the housekeeping department of a dental school. While at work I met a young man who was nice and easy to talk to; so we started to date. Two months after our relationship started, we married. In the back of my mind, I knew it was a mistake. (How many times have you heard someone say, "In the back of my mind . . ."?) I'm beginning to understand that the voice might sound like it's in the back of my mind, but it's really the Lord telling me the *right* thing to do. Even though I did not know Him, He was looking out for me. This young man and I had nothing in common, and we barely knew each other. I think I married as a means of revenge at my mother, who told me not to get married. I learned by experience that marriage is not the way to get back at Mom. Still, I was hoping it would work.

Well, it didn't. After two years of marriage and two sons (Ricky, one year, and Jason, three months), we were filing for divorce. We were just too immature, and we were fighting all the time. While separated, I remember asking my husband for some help with the kids. Out of anger he told me, “I’m not giving you a thing, and don’t call me unless one of them dies.” I know he didn’t mean it, but those words would come back to haunt him in the near future.

I returned to the church where I was raised. In spite of all the pain it caused, I still felt a strong bond. They were like family, however dysfunctional, and the only church I knew. This church taught against divorce, and here I was: a divorced woman with two small boys. I was so ashamed. I knew people would talk, but I made up my mind to put up with it.

It Was the Best of Times; It Was the Worst of Times

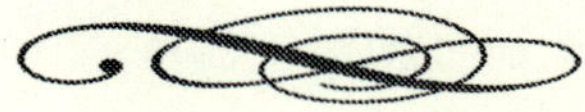

As the deer panteth after the water brooks, so panteth my soul after thee, O God. Psalm 42:1 (KJV)

After being back in church for awhile, I began to talk to a young man at church whom I had known all my life. He and I had dated before I met my first husband. He was wonderful, and I fell in love with him. I believed he loved my boys and me. We married in December 1980. I was so happy, and I just knew God had given me another chance in marriage. My younger son, Jason, was crazy about him, but my older child, Ricky, still needed time to grow used to him. I thought I had married the man of my dreams. Things really seemed to be coming together. Then tragedy struck.

By the end of June 1981, we had been married six months. I was now working as a nursing assistant at a local hospital. My husband and I had to work the weekend, and my mom and dad were out of town. I called one of my girlfriends to see if she could watch the boys for me. She was more than happy to do so. I had one concern, and that was Ricky. He would not stay with anyone but my mother, and I just knew he would give my girlfriend a hard time. When I dropped them off Friday evening to spend the night, I couldn't believe what happened. Jason was the one who didn't want to stay, not Ricky. Jason's reaction shocked me because my girlfriend had watched Jason before and he was never any problem. As I pulled off and turned the corner, I could still hear him crying, "Mommy no, Mommy no!" His crying bothered me so much because it was so unusual for Jason. As soon as I arrived at home, I called to check to see if he was OK. My girlfriend assured me he was OK; in fact, he was standing beside her drinking juice. I felt much better then.

The next day when I went to work, it was such a busy day. At the end of the day, I was so tired I called my girlfriend to let her know I would be picking up the boys soon. She asked if she could keep them overnight, because they were having such a good time. I was so exhausted I agreed. My husband and I went to bed early. At 9:45 P.M., we received a telephone call telling us the boys were hit by a car; while crossing the street with the babysitter. One was taken to University Hospital and the other was taken to Johns Hopkins. They were not able to tell me anything else, just that we needed to hurry. My husband dropped me off at his brother's house, so his brother could take me to University Hospital, while he went to Johns Hopkins.

When we first arrived at University, they could not find either one of the boys. The nurse from University called the nurse at Johns Hopkins to find out where the boys were. The nurse from Johns Hopkins said they had Jason, and she told us Ricky was taken to University. While the staff at University searched for Ricky, the nurse from Johns Hopkins asked to speak to me. I took the telephone and she began to tell me how Jason was doing. She said he was hurt badly and had suffered a fractured skull, but they were doing everything they could for him. As the tears began to flow down my face, I hung up the telephone and just couldn't believe what was happening. By this time they had found Ricky in the adult emergency room. We went in to see Ricky. He suffered some abrasions on his face and his left leg was in a cast, but I knew he would be OK. My mom and dad had arrived by this time.

We left University Hospital to go to see Jason at Johns Hopkins. I couldn't wait to see Jason because I knew Ricky was all right, and I prayed Jason was going to be all right too, in spite of what the nurse said. As we entered the hospital, the security guard told us the pediatric unit was upstairs, and we needed to catch the elevator. When we stepped out of the elevator, I noticed several members of my church and the rest of my family were there. I wondered how they found out so fast about the boys being in the hospital. I was looking for my husband and did not see him. He had left to try to meet me, but we missed each other. I heard them paging him over the hospital intercom, and just then I saw him step out of the elevator. I asked him if he had seen Jason, and he shook his head no. As I looked around the waiting room, I noticed different family members and church members off in corners crying, and I didn't know what was happening. The doctor called us back in the unit. I was so excited, because I couldn't wait to see Jason. The doctor explained that when Jason arrived he had no pulse. They were able to start his pulse again, but he had died five minutes ago. I couldn't believe what I was hearing. This kind of thing only happened to other people, not to us. I experienced a pain I had never felt before, and I can't even describe it. Only a mother who has lost her child can understand this pain.

I was numb and prayed it was just a dream, but it wasn't a dream. I didn't understand why this was happening. I kept having a flashback of the last time I saw Jason, when he was screaming because he didn't want to stay. I started blaming myself for his death. My church's teachings didn't help, because they made me feel that God was punishing me, because I was a divorced woman and had remarried. I thought Jason's death was God's way of punishing me. I was so burdened with guilt. A woman from my church came over to me and told me that Jason's death had nothing to do with my being divorced, which was strange because I had never said that thought out loud. Her words touched my soul, and I knew immediately that God sent her to me. In spite of this assurance, years passed before I could get Jason's scream out of my head. After a week in the hospital, Ricky was discharged and he was just fine.

A month after my son's death, I was scheduled to start nursing school. Several months earlier, I was accepted and all the arrangements were made. Now, I wasn't sure if I would be able to do it. Jason was on my mind, and I was feeling so hurt that I thought I couldn't concentrate enough to be successful. With my husband's strong encouragement, I started. It was pretty rough. At one point I was told I might be put out of the program. Nonetheless, I graduated in January 1984. In February, I was hired at St. Agnes Hospital as a registered nurse.

Once I was out of school, my husband and I decided we were ready for more children. After months and months of trying, we were unsuccessful. Numerous tests conducted on me all came back negative. The doctors decided to test my husband. The day he came home with the news, he was totally devastated. He was the problem. We were put on all kinds of medication. We even tried artificial insemination several times. The process was emotionally and financially draining, and we finally decided not to continue. We thought adoption could be the answer. My husband seemed interested at first, but later he told me he wasn't interested. As a matter of fact, he told me he wasn't interested in having children anymore. At the time, I had no way of knowing how God was orchestrating the circumstances in my life for my benefit. For us, children would have been another tragedy.

As time went on, our sex life deteriorated. I thought it was because of my husband's knowing he was the reason we could not have children. I decided to be patient with him and give him time and space. Things worsened, and I wasn't sure what was happening.

Rumors that my husband was gay were circulating on his job and in the church. Of course, I refused to believe such a thing. He was a deacon in the church and one of the lead singers in the choir, for heaven's sake. These rumors could not be true. One day after I dropped him off at school, I noticed that he left a book in the back seat of the car. I grabbed the book, and a letter fell out that was addressed to him. (He was in the Air Force Reserves and would go away one weekend a month.) This letter, which made reference to the last time he went away on reserve duty, described a sexual encounter between my husband and the writer. I couldn't believe what I was reading. When my husband arrived home that evening, I confronted him with the letter. He denied everything. I not only allowed myself to believe his explanation, I apologized for accusing him in the first place.

I noticed changes in him. He did not go to church as much, and he was not home when he should have been. Several guys were calling the house, and he would never tell me who they were. I began to find more letters and cards from several men. These cards were very sexual, not "thinking of you" or "I'm glad we're friends," but downright intimate. One day I decided to listen in on a conversation between my husband and another man. I could not believe what I was hearing. He was having an affair with this man. Once again, I confronted him, and once again, he denied everything. This time he was physically abusive. From that point on, if I would bring up the topic, I would find myself on the floor.

I was so depressed, I didn't know whether I was coming or going. I would walk around the house screaming and crying. I even thought about suicide but was too scared to go through with it. Who could I talk to about this? Who would believe me? I was already a divorced woman. I knew I was stuck in this situation, so I played the role. I would put a smile on my face for everyone else to see, while my heart was crying on the inside.

One day I was walking through the house praying out loud for God to give me some relief from this heartbreak. Out of nowhere, the face of this older woman in the church came into my mind. Truly God placed this woman in my mind, as I immediately thought of her as someone I could trust. She was indeed a blessing to me, providing comfort and prayers as I confided what was happening to me. I told her I still loved my husband, and I desperately wanted things to work out. Unfortunately, things didn't become any better.

My husband continued to deny his homosexuality. I knew the time had come for me to talk to my mother to make sure she knew what was happening in my marriage. I hadn't told her because I knew it would break her heart. When I told her what was going on, she acted like she was just waiting for me to come to her. I asked her, "How much does God expect us to take?" Without hesitation she said, "God doesn't expect you to take that much."

After ten years of marriage, I realized I couldn't change my husband. In December 1990 in my living room, I raised my hand to God, asking him to deliver me and prepare me for whatever was about to happen. In my mind, only two outcomes were possible; either my husband would change his ways, or he would leave me. In April 1991, God delivered me! My husband moved out to an apartment he had already been renting across town. God knew what had to happen, and at the right time He allowed me to see His answer to my prayer. A year before, his moving would have devastated me, because I was truly devoted to my marriage and I loved my husband. But when he walked out, I felt such peace in my heart. To this day I have not shed a tear. God truly prepared me for that day.

Once again I found myself going through a divorce. I couldn't believe it. I was so ashamed, like I was walking around with two red Ds on my chest. In spite of my feelings, I continued to attend the same church, but my ex-husband stopped attending church altogether. Being in that church was difficult, because part of his family still attended. They did not believe anything I said concerning him. As a matter of fact, his mother accused me of having an affair while married to her son and thought that was the reason he left me. She turned her back on me while I was trying to explain what happened between us. I was so angry with her for what she was saying and doing.

Just When You Think It Can't Get Any Worse

And I said, "Oh that I had wings like a dove! For then would I fly away, and be at rest." Psalm 55:6 (KJV)

After a while, I began to talk to this man at church. His name was Jonathan and I knew his family, but not him. He had just moved back to Baltimore from Hawaii. We became very good friends, so I began to confide in him. He was the only one I could talk to without feeling judged. No one else knew what to say to me or how to counsel me. I just needed someone in my life, other than my family, who wouldn't judge me or make me feel any worse than I already did. We grew closer and closer each day. We became such good friends.

Unfortunately, when word went out that Jonathan and I were talking, the church started buzzing about me again. I remember an older woman in the church saying, "She should give someone else a chance. She's been married twice already." Sometimes I would leave church in tears because of all the talking going on and the coldness I felt from the members. Things became so bad that I would get depressed just walking through the church door. I knew the time had come for me to leave and no longer fellowship there. I also knew this decision would be painful, because I had been in this church most of my life and still felt a bond there.

I continued to talk to Jonathan, and something happened I thought I could never experience again. I fell in love! I believed he loved me as much as I loved him. We married in November 1992. Jonathan was a blessing. He made me feel like a woman again. My second husband left me with such feelings of doubt as a woman that I wasn't sure if I could genuinely love and be loved again. Jonathan referred to me as his queen, and that's just how he treated me. We just seemed to enjoy each other's company. The relationship was so energizing that I would let him talk me into anything. He had me snow skiing, whitewater rafting, swimming in deep water, and just doing anything he wanted me to do. We had so much fun—more fun than I thought possible.

We began to fellowship at a church in Washington, D.C. After a while, Jonathan became the minister of music. While I was at this church, I actually started to truly understand the meaning of salvation. For years I struggled with trying to be perfect, because I thought salvation was based on what I did and how I lived my life. I believed I was expected to live a sin-free life. I can recall people in my old church standing up and testifying that they had not sinned for years. I thought something was wrong with me because I was so imperfect. I never told anyone of this struggle because I was so ashamed.

When I heard the true message of salvation, I realized salvation was not based on what I did, but was available to me because of what Jesus Christ had done on the cross. By shedding *His blood,* He paid for my past, present, and future sins. I learned that I have been sealed in my relationship with Christ, which means *I can't lose my salvation!* Praise God I've been redeemed by His blood, and no one and nothing can pluck me out of His hands. *Hallelujah!* When I came to understand salvation, a burden was lifted—a burden I was carrying for years.

Things really were looking up for me. I had a better understanding of my faith, and I was comfortable in my new church. I was comfortable on my job, working in the operating room, and I was really comfortable in my marriage. Then something started to happen.

Beginning in the later months of 1993, I would get fevers and night sweats at least twice a week. I thought I was just catching some kind of bug. Then I began to feel sick. My temperature was up to 102, and I was having headaches with occasional diarrhea. I thought these symptoms came from stress on my job in the operating room. I went to see my doctor on November 17 and was diagnosed with sinusitis. He started me on antibiotics and Metamucil for diarrhea. I returned to him one week later and reported that I was feeling great.

In January 1994, I decided I needed to gain weight. I weighed 90.8 pounds at the time. Jonathan bought me Ensure to drink, and I was doing well with it. By the next week I was up to 92.4 pounds. I wanted to gain weight because a friend of mine was getting married in May, and I wanted to look good and buy a new outfit for the wedding.

By February 22, I was up to 95.2 pounds, but I started to feel sick again. The fevers would come back every other night. Each day I became weaker and couldn't do everything I used to do. Then I noticed my breathing. If I took a deep breath or yawned, I would feel a funny sensation in my chest that was hard to describe. I wouldn't tell anyone because I was afraid of what they would find. Jonathan would beg me to go to the doctor, but I would refuse.

In March 1994, my health was awful. I had night fevers, shortness of breath, difficulty breathing deeply, and a rash on my face that itched like crazy. As a matter of fact, my whole body itched. On March 4, while at work, I decided to let one of the doctors listen to my lungs. I was leaving for Texas at 7 A.M. the next morning, so I thought I would have some peace of mind if someone would at least listen to my lungs. The doctor told me to take a deep breath. As I breathed in, I began to cough uncontrollably, and then I was very short of breath. The next thing I knew, I was in a wheelchair on my way to the emergency room. No one knew what was wrong. First they thought I had a history of asthma; then they thought one of my lungs collapsed. They started giving me respiratory treatments that helped to open me up, and my breathing became easier. After several treatments I felt better. My X ray was clear, according to the ER doctor, so he diagnosed me with acute bronchitis and started me on prescription drugs. When I knew I was going to be discharged from the ER, I begged my husband to let me go to Texas. After talking to the doctor, he gave in. I went to Texas, and my breathing was better, my skin cleared up, I had no fever, and my appetite increased.

While we were in Texas things were fine, but as we were on our way back home, I noticed my face started to itch again. I blamed the change in atmosphere. On March 14, I went back to see my doctor and get a return-to-work slip. When he saw my rash, he thought I was having an allergic reaction to something. He told me to stop drinking Ensure, and he wanted me to take the braids out of my hair. He also told me to make an appointment with an allergist. My health didn't improve. On March 26 at 4:00 A.M., I woke Jonathan and told him to take me to the ER. This time I was diagnosed with adult-onset asthma, and the doctor started me on two inhalants to help my breathing. He also told me I needed to see a lung specialist.

I made an appointment with Dr. Schultz, who I remembered from when I worked on the hall. The few times I did work with him, I found him to be very pleasant. My appointment was not until April 8. In the meantime, on April 1, I went to Good Friday service, and it was really enjoyable. Toward the end of the service, I started to itch all over, so I forced myself to wait until the service was over, but then left right away. The next day the itching continued, especially on my face. My temperature was up to 102.4. I had some difficulty breathing, and I started coughing. I was feeling so bad I could not go to church on Easter Sunday. My temperature was 101 and I was short of breath, but I went to work on Monday and ended up in the ER at 4:30 P.M. The ER doctor treated me like I was a nut. He wouldn't listen to me; he told me I had nothing serious, and I would be all right. Later the nurse told me the doctor thought my problem was anxiety. Here I was: I'm short of breath, my oxygen level was 67 percent (normal is 85.95 percent), and my temperature was 102.7. How could this man who had never seen me before and didn't ask me any questions about my personal life say the problem was anxiety?

Well, I wasn't admitted, and only God could have worked it out this way: to be admitted in the hospital where I worked would have been a mistake. I'm finding out more and more each day that God's word is true and that "All things work together for good to them that love God, to those who are called according to His purpose" (Romans 8:28). Praise God who's helping me, when I don't know how to help myself.

I had four more days before my appointment with Dr. Schultz.

It's Aids

Then Job arose, and rent his mantle, and shaved his head, and fell down upon the ground, and worshipped, and said; "Naked came I out of my mother's womb, and naked shall I return thither; the Lord gave, and the Lord hath taken away; blessed be the name of the Lord." Job 1:20–21 (KJV)

I didn't think I would make it to see Dr. Schultz. When I went in, he examined me and he looked at my X ray. First, he told me my X ray was not normal. Later he examined my rash and asked me to describe the symptoms I was having. He told me he thought I had this disease called sarcoidosis stage 3. He said this disease usually occurs in black women my age with the same symptoms. No one knew that, in my heart, I was relieved with that diagnosis. He said he was 99 percent sure, but wanted me to have a CAT scan done, a biopsy of my chin, and lots of blood work. I only weighed 88 pounds at this visit. He said that once all my results came back, he would start me on Prednisone for nine months, which should make me feel better.

Something strange happened as I was leaving his office. He called me back in and closed the door. He asked if there was any chance that I was HIV-positive. I told him I had no drug history, but that I had been married several times and one of my husbands was gay. He asked me if he could draw a HIV blood test, and I agreed. He set up an appointment to see me in ten days, the longest ten days of my life. I prayed and begged God to let the test come back negative. I remembered praying what Jesus prayed in the garden, "O my Father, if it be possible, let this cup pass from me . . ." (Matthew 26:39).

As I waited for my appointment on April 20, I would lie in bed praying that my test results would be negative. One night I woke up, opened my nursing journals, and began to compare the signs and symptoms of sarcoidosis with HIV. Each time I compared, I would fall under the HIV heading. In the back of my mind, I just knew I was HIV-positive, but I was still hoping. The morning of April 20 came. For some strange reason I decided to look at the back of my throat. When I saw the white spots in there, I knew for sure that I was HIV-positive.

My brother, David, picked me up to take me to the doctor's office. My mother and father waited at my place to hear the diagnosis. I told Jonathan to just go to work and everything would be OK, but I was really scared. We arrived at the doctor's office early. I only waited about ten minutes before he called me in. He told me the CAT scan confirmed what he thought (sarcoidosis), but they couldn't find my blood work and the chin biopsy was not done. Because he didn't have all the test results back, he wanted to set up another appointment.

Just when he was about to schedule me for another appointment, the blood work results came in. Dr. Schultz looked at them, straightened the paper, and then turned to something on the other side of his desk. It was like he didn't know what to do next. Then he asked me if I had a few minutes. I said yes, not knowing what he was about to tell me. He said, "Alice, I don't know how to tell you this, but you are HIV-positive."

Even though I knew, I still didn't want to believe it. I sat across from him with tears in my eyes. I felt, in that short period of time, my life had changed forever. I thought, *I'm going to die! I'm going to lose my job! People will reject me and no one will want to be around me! I'm going to get sicker and sicker and lose even more weight!* Out of all that, what bothered me most was being rejected.

Dr. Schultz decided he needed to do a bronchoscope, and he was arranging for the procedure to be done at the St. Agnes Hospital operating room. At this point, I wasn't ready for my job to know. When I brought this fact to his attention, he realized that going to St. Agnes was not a good idea. He made all the arrangements for me to have the procedure done at Baltimore County Hospital. He had a friend who was a pulmonary surgeon there. Dr. Schultz and his office personnel were very supportive and took care of everything. As I was about to leave the office he hugged me, telling me how sorry he was for me, and that he was sad because I was an innocent victim.

My brother was still in the waiting room, and I wasn't sure how I would tell him. He knew something was wrong because he heard them calling out my name while they were making arrangements for me to have the tests done. While the secretary was making a copy of my chart to take to Baltimore County Hospital, I sat beside my brother and wrote on a piece of paper "HIV+." He didn't know what to say. I could tell he was hurt, and I knew he would be supportive. I remember leaving the doctor's office, but I don't remember ever getting in the car. I do remember my brother rubbing my head and telling me it was going to be all right.

As we were on our way home, I was wondering how I was going to tell my mom and dad. They were back at the apartment waiting. I really didn't want to tell them because I wasn't sure what the news would do to them. I wanted to protect them from the pain. When I entered the apartment, they were sitting there. I wasn't ready to tell just yet, so I told them I was going to call Jonathan from my room and I would talk to them later. I called Jonathan and told him the news. I could hear in his voice that he was shocked. I remembered when I told him my suspicion that I might be diagnosed as HIV-positive, he told me I would not be. He was so sweet and supportive. He told me he would come home as soon as he could.

Mother and Daddy were still waiting patiently. I walked out to the kitchen and announced I was HIV-positive. I was waiting for hysteria and tears, but instead I saw a strength in both of them I never saw before. My mother said, "Well, OK, that's what the doctors say, but I serve a God and nothing is impossible with Him." My father sat quietly. I was relieved because I could tell they would be all right.

After I told my parents, I went to my room to lie down. I was still very sick and extremely depressed. All I could do was wonder how God expected me to deal with yet another major trial in my life. Not only was I going to die, but I was going to die from a disease people labeled as horrible as leprosy. I couldn't understand why He would choose this form of illness to take my life.

As I lie in bed with tears in my eyes, I started thinking about one of my coworkers. We worked together in the operating room. She had a horrible reputation at the hospital for having such a negative attitude. Later, I came to know the other workers in the hospital labeled her for things she had done in the past. As she and I began to develop a relationship, I learned she was a Christian. She took me under her wing, and in tough times she would pray with me. One day she shared with me that her nephew had been diagnosed with AIDS. I could see the compassion in her eyes as she shared how she cared for him. I prayed she would call me. I needed someone to confide in, and I knew I could trust her.

Clearly God had placed her in my life, and He was orchestrating my circumstances for His purposes. I thought how good it would be for me to talk to her. A couple of hours later my phone rang. It was her! I started sharing with her all the doctor had said to me. As I cried over the phone, she started ministering to me and praying for me. I knew I had made the right decision in opening up to her. I could tell she was going to be there for me. After our conversation, I felt much better and drifted off to sleep. After Jonathan came home that night, he just sat and held me. He said we would be all right. I knew he was going to go through this with me all the way. I thank God for him.

The next day I had to go for blood work and a chin biopsy. I had the blood work done at Baltimore County Hospital. The technicians were very nice. I went to a private dermatologist to have my chin biopsy. I watched the receptionist as she pulled out my chart. The first thing I saw was "HIV+," and it was circled. I felt marked for life. Everyone in the office was extremely pleasant, despite the stigma, and I was grateful for that.

In working with medical professionals, I knew the horrible stigma attached to AIDS patients. I remembered a time on the hall when nurses would refuse to work with AIDS patients. In the operating room, I would see some staff members excessively gown and glove themselves if they knew an AIDS patient was coming. Seeing how some of the medical staff would reject AIDS patients was always very troubling to me. Ironically I was one of only a few nurses who had no problem working with AIDS patients. Little did I know that one day someone would have to take care of me because I had AIDS.

On April 22 I was scheduled for a bronchoscope. My mother and my brother Mickey took me to the hospital. I felt awful. I could hardly walk. As we entered the hospital, an elderly volunteer led us to the location where the procedure would be performed. My mother asked her to slow down because I couldn't keep up. That walk seemed like the longest of my life, and I remember thinking I would not go home tonight. As we arrived, an old nurse was waiting for me. She asked the volunteer my name.

When the volunteer announced my name, the nurse ran back to the room and returned with a mask. Right in the middle of the hall she slapped it on me, without warning. Her action left me feeling so humiliated, but I knew she was just doing her job. She placed me in a room, and then she left. The next nurse who came was very pleasant. She and another nurse brought a lounge chair so I could lie back. I couldn't believe she was so nice to me. As I sat there, I heard a man's voice—Dr. White's—asking for me. I heard the nurse offer him a mask, and he asked if I was actively coughing. She told him no, so he refused the mask. He entered my room, introduced himself, and shook my hand. He apologized for the way the mask was slapped on me and explained it was hospital policy to isolate AIDS patients who are having difficulty breathing, because it could be a sign of tuberculosis.

After the doctor's examination, the nurse from the operating room came to get me. She helped me onto the stretcher and asked why I was having a bronchoscope. I told her what happened, and she told me she was so sorry. She rolled me down the hall to the operating room, joking with me and trying to get me to laugh. People just don't know how far a simple act of kindness goes to ease the anxiety and tension patients feel, especially AIDS patients.

The next thing I remember is waking up in the recovery room coughing and short of breath. My brother was on one side and my mother was on the other. I felt awful. I knew I was not going home. The nurse came in to take my temperature, which was 102.7. I could hear her say there was no way I was going home. I felt so bad, I just wanted to be left alone. It was now 6:30 P.M., and they were ready to take me to my room. I told my brother to take my mother home. She had been there all day and had not eaten. I told them both I would be all right.

My mother and brother left, and I was moved to my room. All I wanted was to sleep and be alone. They asked me if I wanted the phone and TV turned on; I said no. I didn't want to see anyone or talk to anyone. As a matter of fact, I chose to just lie in bed with my head covered. I was afraid someone would come in my room and recognize me, and I wasn't ready to see rejection. The nurses would come in to give me medication and then leave. They would roll my meal tray in and just leave it; no one offered to help me. I remember thinking, *Boy, nursing has really changed!* Later I realized people were reacting to the way I was behaving. Sometimes as patients, we don't realize we are sending messages to others, who modify their behavior based on what they see us doing.

The infectious control doctor came to see me. He was very pleasant and told me I was not alone. He sensed I was depressed and had a negative frame of mind. He said that how much medication I took or how much I changed my diet didn't matter; if I couldn't change my attitude, the disease would progress quicker. I asked him where I was in the disease. He explained to me that they decide by looking at my CD4 count. Normal is over 1000; AIDS is 200 and below. Then he told me my count was 18. I couldn't believe it. I had full-blown AIDS.

Jonathan came in later and fed me. I didn't even want him to stay. He asked me about the TV and phone, and again I said no. I just wanted to be alone. That night, all I could do was wonder *why?* I couldn't understand what I did that was so bad to deserve this. My whole life had changed in seconds.

I had a rough night. I couldn't move without becoming short of breath. I was up every hour, going to the bathroom, which was such a struggle.

Healing Relationships

"Come unto me, all ye that labour and are heavy laden; and I will give you rest. Take my yoke upon you, and learn of me; for I am meek and lowly in heart; and ye shall find rest unto your souls." Matthew 11:28–29 (KJV)

The second day in the hospital, as I lay in bed there was a knock on my door. Dina and her husband walked into the room, and I was shocked. I never expected her to come to the hospital; I was truly touched. I'd only known her for two years, and she just took me under her wing. She hugged me and told me she had everyone praying for me. She opened her Bible and began to read Mark 5:25—the story of the woman with an "issue of blood." Then she said, "Now Alice, this woman has been sick longer than you, but when she touched the hem of Jesus' garment, she was made whole." She explained how the touching of Jesus' garment represented her faith. I was so encouraged, I could feel my spirit lifting. Her husband told me to keep my chin up, and before they left, they prayed for me.

There was another knock on my door. I saw a man, and as he entered I realized it was my sister-in-law's pastor, Pastor Brooks. The first thing he said was, "Privacy is one thing, but this is ridiculous." (I still had the door closed, the blinds closed, and the lights dim.) "Put some light in this room and open the blinds so the sun can shine in." He went on to say, "Don't you know Satan loves darkness, and he will use it to work on your mind?" All I could do was laugh because I knew he was right. He came to my bedside and asked me what was wrong. I told him I was HIV-positive. He said, "OK, but you're going to be all right."

He went on to say, "Once you get your strength back, I want you to think about something." Then he asked, "Where will you go from here? Are you going to use this to help someone, or to glorify God or what?" I really did not want to hear or even to think about anything other than the horrible condition I was experiencing. How could I think about glorifying God, when all I could think about was that I am going to die? How could God get the glory out of this? However, his questions shook me up. He prayed for me and left. I couldn't get his questions out of my head. At that point, I decided I would come out of the dark; I had Jonathan open up everything.

I also decided not to blame anyone. I knew nothing could happen to me that God didn't allow. This illness happened for a reason. I can't begin to know why He allowed it, but He did. Then I began waiting on God to direct me in the way He wanted me to go. I started feeling better, even though the nights were still rough.

The next day, the doctor discontinued my oxygen. I was still short of breath, but the doctor said my O_2 level was good. Jonathan's brother, André, and his wife, Barbara, came to see me with flowers. In no time, they had me laughing so hard I thought I would go into respiratory distress. I really enjoyed their visit, and I knew they were in my corner. They had prayer with me, and as they were leaving they asked if I wanted the door closed. I said, "*No!*"

I had Jonathan contact a few people for me. First, I had him call my cousin Keven, who was always special to me, and who had always been there for me. He came over right away. When I told him I was HIV-positive, he got down on his knees, held my hand, and asked what I needed him to do. He was always so supportive. Next, Jonathan called, Kathy, a woman I worked with in labor and delivery. She, too, came over right away. She sat on the bed and held my hand. I told her the diagnosis and she started to cry. She was crying so badly, I tried to console her. She couldn't stop crying, and I remember thinking, *This white girl is crying over me!* She stayed with me for a while and helped me with my food. I told her I didn't want anyone at the hospital to know yet, and she promised to say nothing until I was ready. I thanked God for her.

At this point, the doctors decided to transfuse me because my blood count was too low, which they believed could explain my shortness of breath. When Jonathan came to see me, I was so short of breath and weak I couldn't talk. I motioned to him that I couldn't, so he just sat down and held my hand. Later he walked around the bed, laid across me, and began to cry. He said, "Please get better. I can't live without you." After a few days, I began to feel better and was ready to be discharged. Jonathan was so happy. As the nurse rolled me out the door, the sun shone in my face, and the weather was beautiful. I thanked God for life and for the breath of fresh air he sent to my dark hospital room. I was so grateful for the Christian friends and relatives who wouldn't let me dwell on my circumstances. Instead, God led them to challenge me to step into the light of His love and be energized by it.

Not long after my discharge from the hospital, I asked Jonathan to contact my head nurse so I could discuss my job. She came over that night, brought a pair of pajamas, and gave me a big hug. I told her my diagnosis, and she said she was so sorry for me. She assured me they would find some place for me to work in the hospital and told me she would be there if I needed anything. The next day she called me, after speaking to the employee health nurse, and told me not to worry. She said I was not obligated to tell anyone about my condition, and that I could continue to work in the operating room. She went on to tell me to call her if I needed counseling, so she could make those arrangements. I was so excited when I hung up the phone. I remember thinking, *This is unbelievable. God has worked everything out, and I don't have to give up nursing!* I thought for sure I could no longer be a nurse. What a mighty God, who lifts burdens and makes all things possible!

I recall reading a daily devotional entitled "On Purpose," which explained how no accidents take place in the lives of God's children. Our misfortunes are not accidents, nor are they the work of an unloving God. The devotional said, "What looks like just an accident, when viewed through human eyes, is really God at work in us; His blessing in disguise. God Transforms Trials into Triumphs." The devotional left me an appreciation of the need for FAITH. I had to decide if I was going to spend the rest of my life questioning God or trusting Him. I decided:

F orsaking
A ll
I
T rust
H im.

As time went by, I prayed and asked God to put a special person in my life. I needed someone who could relate to my condition and provide some support. Esther, a close friend I grew up with at church, called to tell me about a seminar she attended on HIV/AIDS. She thought it was so incredible that the speaker was someone I knew, Diane Powell. Esther gave me Diane's telephone number and said I should give her a call. Once again, God let me know He was with me. He sent someone who was HIV-positive, saved, and a woman. Praise God!

I called Diane, who invited me to her home the next day. As I pulled up to her home, I could not believe my eyes. This little woman came out to meet me. It was Diane! I could see how her body had deteriorated from AIDS. She was so thin, she didn't have much hair, and she was very weak. I was startled, so I had to quickly pull myself together so she wouldn't notice my response. We sat in the living room, and she asked what she could do for me. I told her I just wanted someone to talk to, and she shared her story. In spite of her physical condition, I noticed that she seemed content and satisfied. She talked about the goodness of God. I saw a power in her life that was real and strong. She was very warm and compassionate. I was so glad to see her again. As I continued to visit Diane, I felt she was doing much more for me than the doctors. Her health continued to fail, but her trust in God grew stronger.

On one visit, Diane told me she would not be around long and that I should continue where she left off. I was not ready to hear this. I could not at that point speak out on AIDS. I was not as bold and not nearly as strong as Diane. Yet, every time I saw her she would push me to speak out. I spoke to a couple of close friends and confided to them what Diane was telling me to do. One said I shouldn't run away from it, but I shouldn't jump into it either. Another friend told me, "God can use us best when we think we're too weak or unworthy." I didn't know what I should do. I decided to wait.

My God, My God, Why Have You Forsaken Me?

Wither shall I go from thy spirit? Or wither shall I flee from thy presence? If I ascend up into heaven, thou art there; if I make my bed in hell, behold, thou art there. Psalm 139:7–8 (KJV)

In May 1995, we decided to move out of our apartment and buy a house. Not very long after the move, Jonathan started experiencing abdominal pain. Our neighbor teased him and said it was probably from looking at the debt he'd taken on. When the pain became worse, I took him to the doctor and they ran all kinds of tests.

I took him back and forth so many times, and each time we would get a different diagnosis.

Unbelievably, in the midst of all this trouble the unthinkable happened. Esther called to tell me that Diane was dead! The one I asked God to bring into my life, the person who I became so close to and could identify with my illness, was gone. I told people I had the greatest support system anyone could ask for: Jonathan, Diane, and my family. With all that was happening to Jonathan, I barely had time to grieve for my dear friend. I guess I thought I would create that space once Jonathan was better. Little did I know what was in store.

Finally, I took Jonathan to a specialist. He was diagnosed with cancerous tumors in the lower part of his pelvis and needed to start radiation therapy right away. We switched roles: I was now taking care of him. I took him back and forth to the hospital for his radiation treatments every day for about two weeks. He was not responding to the radiation treatments, so they decided to do surgery. Immediately after the surgery, Jonathan began to improve and I was able to take him home, but this improvement didn't last long. He started having breathing problems. Once again, I took him back and forth to the hospital while they treated him for pneumonia, but he continued to have breathing difficulty. They took another X ray, which showed some changes. The following sequence of events were so incredible, I felt like I was in someone else's nightmare.

On Monday, August 21, the doctors performed a bronchoscope. On Tuesday, August 22, the doctor came into Jonathan's room with the nurse. He said Jonathan did not have pneumonia. Instead, tumors in the lower part of his pelvis had spread to his lungs; nothing else could be done. I couldn't believe my ears. Tears flowed down my face as if being poured from a fountain. As I positioned myself next to Jonathan, he told me not to worry; he would be all right. He told me to go home and that he would call me to say goodnight. I never got that call.

Wednesday, August 23: I went to the hospital early to check on Jonathan. I noticed as I was coming down the hall that medical staff was running into his room. When I reached the door, I could see them working on him. One of the nurses grabbed me and took me into the lounge. She said I needed to call the family because things did not look good. I stayed with Jonathan all night. So many friends and family members were there, and I needed the support. Jonathan was in so much pain that they started a morphine drip. Watching him suffer was so painful. Occasionally, he would look up at me and ask me to help him, but I felt so helpless.

Thursday, August 24: I looked into Jonathan's eyes and realized I needed to let him go. As soon as I told the nurses to leave him alone, I held him to let him know I was ready. Jonathan took his last breath, as if God was waiting for me to accept His Will before He took Jonathan away.

I was incredibly heartsick. I was ready to give up. If this loss was the only one in my life, it couldn't have hurt any more. I had experienced a failed marriage, Jason's death, learning my husband was gay, being diagnosed with AIDS, Diane's death, and now the death of my current husband—the one who was going to take care of me and be there for me. I just wanted to die. Days turned into weeks and weeks into months, but the pain never ceased. I would go out and put a smile on my face, but my heart was so broken. I just cried in bed all night. I was all alone, and my hurt was unbearable. I asked God to take me, but each morning I would wake up.

I didn't understand why I had to endure so much loss in my life. Why didn't God just let me go to be with Jonathan? I know people aren't supposed to question God, but my heart hurt. I thought God would be merciful by letting me leave this world. I was dying anyway!

In November, I was experiencing signs of pneumonia. I remember lying in bed and struggling with my breathing. Ricky was in the next room asleep, but I didn't want to upset him. As my breathing became more difficult, I knew I was going to die. After all these weeks and months of wanting to die, I finally found myself faced with death. Then I realized I did not want to die. I remember praying, *Lord, not now. I want to live.* As my breathing continued to worsen, another fear came over me. I was dying alone.

A book about angels was on my nightstand, and I just had the urge to pick it up. As I scanned through the book, I noticed a chapter on angels and death. God ministered to me through that book, because it explained that I would not be alone when my time to die comes. God will dispatch His angels to me, and with smiling faces they will cheerfully carry me home. God's word says not to fear because I am never alone, even in death. With tears of joy streaming down my face, I peacefully fell asleep.

The next morning I awoke and thanked God for another day and for life; yes, for life! As I looked at the tragedies in my life, I could see a pattern. Each time, after the tragedy, I came to know God better and understand how He is and how much He loves me. I recalled the story of Joseph in the Old Testament. As Joseph examined his life, with all its trials and tragedies, he said something profound. He thought about his brothers' abuse, being sold into slavery and accused of sexual assault. When given an opportunity to confront his brothers with their misdeeds, and having the authority to make them pay, he said, "You meant it for evil, but God meant it for good." I also read, "It was good for me to be afflicted so that I might learn your statutes" (Psalm 119:71).

At this point I was beginning to understand. God knew what was going to happen to me, and He let it happen. If He let it happen, then He has a plan to bring me through it. I needed to stop focusing on my pain and choose to let God pull me through my trials. I trust Him enough to know I'll grow in my faith and, as a result, be more useful to Him.

Through My Child's Eyes

Jesus saith unto him, "Rise, take up thy bed, and walk." John 5:8 (KJV)

If this chapter seems like an abrupt turn to you, the suddenness expresses just how abruptly it occurred to me that I was so caught up in my circumstances, and not in touch with what was going on with my son. You may recall I had two sons. Jason was the one who died, and Ricky survived the accident with a fractured leg and several abrasions. Ricky is quite healthy now and is in a doctoral program. I will give him an opportunity to share what was happening with him while I was caught up in my troubles.

* * *

Hello, my name is Richard M. Smith. My mom wanted me to share with you what was happening with me, in my own words.

When my brother died, I was confused. I was three years old. When I saw Jason after the accident, he looked like he was sleeping in a fancy bed. He had a white sailor's suit, and he was lying very still. I wanted him to get up to play with me, but he wouldn't.

We had fun with each other. I remember us taking a frying pan, putting nails in it, placing it on the stove, and pretending we were cooking. Another time we were sitting on the hard wood floor at my grandmother's house, and we poured flour on the floor and played in it. I can't remember if we got into any trouble for that. I don't remember too much else, except I couldn't understand why he wouldn't get up out of that fancy bed and play with me. I touched his arm, hoping to wake him, but he would not wake up. I think of him now and then. I wonder what he would be like if he were still alive. However, I take comfort in knowing he is in a better place and knowing he's watching over me.

I don't remember my birth father. My mother's second husband raised me. As a matter of fact, I thought he was my birth father, until I read the front of my mother's Bible, where I saw my mother and her second husband were married after I was born. My mother explained the situation and tried to get me to remember the adoption. I vaguely remembered talking with a judge; I was just too young to understand what was happening.

As I was growing up, I thought everything was pretty normal and happy. I had a lot of respect for my dad, because he reminded me of my grandfather, strong and quiet. I saw him as a superhero who took care of his family, kept order, kept us safe, and applied discipline.

I didn't see the divorce coming. It hit me out of nowhere. I remember one day my dad didn't come home. Mom said he would come over the next day to talk to me, but he didn't come. Mom told me about the separation, and I was so very sad. When my dad did talk to me, he would make it sound like the separation was temporary, and he was working on being a better father to me.

On the other hand, my mom made it clear after my dad left that he was not going to come back. For some time I was upset with my mom because I thought she should try to get my dad to come back home, and she wasn't trying at all. After about a year, my mom explained how my dad's lifestyle was the reason for the separation, and they were getting a divorce.

At first I was confused. This man taught me how to play baseball. He was the one who told me to stop crying and get back on my bicycle after I busted my knee. He had always been a masculine authority figure in my life, and I was hurt to learn he was gay.

When my mom started dating Jonathan, I didn't like him at all. I thought he was coming into my mom's life when she was very vulnerable, and I believed he was taking advantage of her. He tried to be a friend to me. After they were married; he tried to be a father. He taught me how to drive and we eventually connected in some fashion. It seemed as though he and I battled for my mother's affection. When Mom got sick, we both would try to be there for her; she chose him.

Seeing my mom in the hospital was hard; she was so pale and could barely breathe. I remember one day I called her before coming to the hospital; her voice sounded so terrible because she was having difficulty breathing and talking. I was too uncomfortable to go to see her. When she told me she had AIDS, I was so devastated that I went to my room and cried for several days.

As a senior in high school, carrying around the knowledge that my mom had AIDS was somewhat difficult. My mom told my school principal, all of my teachers, and my coach. I didn't tell any of my peers for quite some time. As a matter of fact, my best friend saw my mom doing a TV show about AIDS and called me to ask if there was something I wanted to tell him. I was comfortable with my mom's choice to tell people about her condition, but at school I would hear kids talking about people with AIDS in brutal ways. Kids had stereotyped people with AIDS as being homosexuals or drug users; my mom was neither of these. One time I was sitting in class during a discussion about AIDS. A young man said all people with AIDS should be rounded up and shipped far away from civilization. I became so angry that I was about to hit this guy, but my teacher jumped in and settled the situation down.

Seemingly out of nowhere, Jonathan's death was a major shock. Things were beginning to settle down; I had just been with him in the hospital the day before. He told me, "They don't think I'm going to make it, but I'm going to be all right." The next day he was dead, and I couldn't believe it. He was not sick very long, and I had no clue how sick he was until it was too late. I can recall, at one point, thinking he was just trying to attract attention. His death saddened me, mostly because of seeing my mom so devastated.

After Jonathan's death, Mom got sick again. Living alone with her was hard, as sick as she was. The difficulty was mostly because of my mom waiting until she couldn't breathe before she would go to the hospital. I walked around the house paranoid every time I heard her coughing. I was always running to her room to make sure she was OK. My grandmother told me to tell my mom I was the man of the house, so she should listen to me and do what I said. No one knew how stubborn Mom was; she would do anything to keep from going to the hospital.

Mom got back on her feet somewhat. I think she was being strong just for my sake so we could go to college fairs and make college visits. She had her good days and bad days. I think it was important to her that I was comfortable leaving for college. By this time, Mom had become so comfortable telling people she had AIDS. She would talk about it while we were visiting colleges. I wasn't quite ready for that. Mom would be talking to the president of a college, and before you know it, she would turn and point me out as her son, which was soon after she told the college president she had AIDS. I supported Mom's discussing AIDS, but I remember thinking, *My goodness, Mom, can you wait until I've been accepted at a school before you tell everybody?*

In college, I was less private about my mom's condition. I tended to wait and check out how open-minded someone was before I shared Mom's condition, but I really didn't care who knew it. In my junior year, I invited Mom to speak about AIDS at my school. She did a great job; I only wish more students were there to hear it.

I'm in a doctoral program now, and I couldn't be more proud of how my mom is using her experiences to help others. She is a wonderful role model of someone who has accepted her life's circumstances and made something positive come out of it. As she says, "You can suck on a lemon, or you can make lemonade."

A Charge to Keep

"Go ye therefore, and teach all nations, baptizing them in the name of the Father, and of the Son, and of the Holy Ghost; teaching them to observe all things whatsoever I have commanded you. . . ." Matthew 28:19–20a (KJV)

Once I got my head on straight, I stopped focusing on my pain. One of the first things I needed to do was find a church for study and fellowship; however, I wanted to do it on my own terms. I just wanted a place where I could attend regularly and just ease in and out; I didn't want to be a member anywhere. A friend of mine told me of a church in the area called Colonial

Baptist Church. The good thing about it was they had a 9:30 A.M. worship service. I liked that because 8 A.M. was too early and 11 A.M. was too late for me. Ricky and I attended, and both of us thought the service was beautiful. However, at the end of the service they announced the 9:30 service was being discontinued. We decided to go to the 8 A.M. service; after a couple weeks, for some reason, we just didn't feel the same and we stopped attending.

The next several Sundays we attended other churches we had previously visited. I noticed Ricky was not very comfortable. I wanted to find a church that was not only sound in Bible teaching, but also a church that had something Ricky could become involved in and excited about. I couldn't push Colonial Baptist Church out of my mind, so we went back there and this time attended the 11 A.M. service. It was wonderful. I was most impressed with how I could experience a genuine feeling of love when I entered the door. They didn't know me—and they certainly didn't know what I had been through—but I was still greeted with love each time I went there.

During one of our visits, they announced that a course called "Experiencing God" was about to start. That topic sounded like something I would enjoy, but I didn't know if I could participate since I wasn't a member. I asked one of the ladies at the registration desk if I could sign up and she said yes. My prayer was to know God better and be used for His purpose. As I became involved in the study, what it means to experience God became clearer to me. I was so thankful for this gift of a deeper understanding of God and His word.

My first realization was that I was more self-centered than God-centered. I needed to be more in touch with the fact that God didn't need me; I needed Him. I realized if I focused more on God and what He was doing, then what I needed to do would become clearer. At that time, what I needed to do was to be still and know God better. As a case in point, I had struggled for a year about going to the HIV support group that my healthcare provider offered. My feeling was that I was not a typical AIDS patient. I knew the groups were going to be made up of drug addicts and gay men, and I couldn't relate to them. However, I just felt compelled to attend the group even though I could see no value in it. I decided to go to a session and prayed for God to go with me to get me through it. Different members spoke about their issues. Then one young lady, with tears in her eyes, spoke. She said she was extremely depressed because she was HIV-positive and her husband died recently. I could feel her pain because I had been through what she was going through. I knew God had led me there, and I knew why. I shared my story with her and the group. I let them know that my hope, my peace, my joy, and my comfort was in Jesus Christ. I had an opportunity to minister to the young lady, and I experienced the presence of God.

Every pain I ever felt, every experience I ever had, every trial, every tragedy all led to that moment when I could see how God was ordering my steps to this place at this time. As I continued in study, I was challenged by God's word: "Trust in the Lord with all thine heart and lean not to thine own understanding. In all thy ways acknowledge Him and He will direct thy path" (Proverbs 3:5–6). God's plan for me to move out of my comfort zone, trust Him, and let Him use me became crystal clear.

My younger brother, Arthur, asked me if I would speak on HIV/AIDS to a youth group of about two hundred people at his church. My initial response was yes. However, as the time drew near I was developing cold feet. Again, I had to remember the experience in the support group and trust God to get me through. I prayed for God to use me, if only to keep one teenager from walking in my shoes. The talk was a blessing. Not only did I teach them about AIDS, but I also let them know that Christ made the difference in my life. After my talk, so many teenagers came up and thanked me for sharing my story. One girl told me she had been struggling with getting involved with risky behaviors and that she was about to do it. When she heard me speak, she knew God had sent me and she was no longer going to go through with it. I was truly blessed.

At that moment, I understood that the compelling force that led me to the support group was the same force that gave me confidence to speak to those young people. God orchestrated the circumstances; all He wanted was for me to be obedient enough so He could show me how He wanted to use me. I promised Him I would lift up His name every chance I could and be available to minister to anyone He placed in my path.

After being diagnosed with AIDS, I saw where God brought me from and how He pulled me through. All my doctors told me to get my affairs in order because I wasn't going to last one year. In 1996, two years after my diagnosis, I was speaking out. God was using me—simple, ordinary me—to tell people of the hope in Jesus Christ. I remember when Diane Powell told me that she would not be around long and that I had to continue the work. I thought she was out of her mind. I realized God was shaping me for my ministry. He allowed my struggles to help me grow.

A Healing Environment

"If ye abide in me, and my words abide in you, ye shall ask what ye will, and it shall be done unto you." John 15:7 (KJV)

In April 1996, my gynecologist called to tell me my PAP smear was abnormal and he needed to repeat it. He said he couldn't be sure if there were cancerous cells or if the virus was in my cervix. I remember putting down the phone and thinking the virus was beginning to break down other parts of my body. Suddenly, I became anxious and felt burdened. I prayed and asked God to do His will and said I would trust Him, no matter what the outcome. I shared this news with a friend, who responded by saying Satan was angry with me. I asked her to explain. She said since I'm working for God—studying His Word and speaking out for Jesus—the enemy was coming after me. She insisted Satan was trying to steal my joy so I would become distracted and take my focus away from praising God, serving God, and seeking His will. Instead, I would start looking at my circumstances, stay anxious about my condition, and lose sight of my ministry.

I heard a minister explain it using a boxing metaphor. He said the boxer needs to keep his gloves up to protect his face and head. The opponent will work on his exposed body, causing the boxer to lower his gloves and leaving his face and head exposed. The opponent sees the opportunity to knock him out, so he proceeds to hit him in the head. I understood that as long as I was focused on God, my gloves were up and I was protected. However, if I allowed fear, doubt, and disbelief to set in, I would lower my gloves and give Satan a clear shot at my head.

The boxing illustration caused me to identify an area where I needed to make a commitment. I needed to become a member at the church where God had led me. I extended the boxing metaphor to help me appreciate my spiritual need. I needed a trainer (pastor) to guide me and give me benefit of his wisdom and experience. I needed a corner team (brothers and sisters) to watch me work and give me tips on how to be more effective. I needed a roadwork regimen (Bible study) to stay sharp and fit for the competition. I needed a sparring partner (prayer partner) to help me strengthen and enhance my skills. OK, enough boxing.

I saw the necessity of being in an environment where I was challenged to keep my guard up against the enemy. I went back to Colonial Baptist Church. I knew God was leading me to join, but I resisted. I thought the church was too big, and they didn't have a full-time pastor in place. I used so many excuses. One Sunday the minister preached about all the excuses Moses used for not being the one to lead the people of Israel. That message convicted me to get off my butt and make a commitment. As a matter of fact, the entire week I heard messages about commitment. I felt God was saying, "Trust Me," so I did. I became a member of Colonial on Mother's Day, May 12, 1996.

Be Still and See the Power of God

"Behold, I will do a new thing, now it shall spring forth; shall ye not know it? I will even make a way in the wilderness, and rivers in the desert." Isaiah 43:19 (KJV)

Since my diagnosis in 1994, my prayer wasn't to live a long life or to receive a miraculous healing. My heartfelt desire was to see my son graduate from high school. Well, I have seen Ricky graduate from high school and college, marry a wonderful young lady, and he is currently in a doctoral program studying to be a sociology professor. One scripture that comes to mind is, "Now unto Him, Who is able to do exceeding abundantly above all that we ask or think, according to the power that worketh in us . . ." (Ephesians 3:20).

After I joined Colonial, my health was not much better. The GYN doctor found precancerous cells in subsequent PAP smears. He suggested removing part of the cervix in September 1996. I had just started attending the women's Bible study class. I only went to the class to keep a commitment I made to my new membership class teacher; I did not intend to stay. I enjoyed the class and decided to return. Little did I know how God had planned to use my Sunday school teacher, Eileen. She would become my dearest friend and a support person in my time of greatest need.

The Sunday before my procedure, I told the class about the procedure and asked them to pray for me. I explained what was involved and told them the doctor suspected cervical cancer. I could see a look of genuine concern on their faces. I don't know quite what possessed me to say, "Well, if you think that's something, it's nothing compared to the fact I was diagnosed with AIDS in 1994." They responded in a very supportive way. The day before the procedure, Eileen and her sister Sandy came over to my house to have prayer with me and ask if they could do anything. I was particularly touched by Eileen's response, because so many times I've heard people tell me they would be there for me, but they were always walking away when they said it. I also heard people say I should let them know what they can do for me, and the difficulty is that I don't feel comfortable saying I just need someone to spend time with me. What made my relationship with Eileen so special was that she just showed up and spent some time with me. I would never have asked someone to do that.

After the GYN procedure, I developed pneumonia symptoms. I saw the doctor and was given some medication to take at home, because he knew I didn't want to be admitted again. However, my condition didn't get any better and I had a lot of trouble breathing. Saturday night the nurse called and tried to convince me to come in, but I told her I would wait until Monday. On

Sunday I told my class I was going into the hospital on Monday and asked them to pray for me again. Later that evening, Eileen and Sandy stopped by my house to see me. They visited for some time and then prayed for me before they left. My breathing got so bad, I couldn't wait until Monday. I was admitted that night. This was my fourth time being admitted for pneumonia. The doctors were very concerned because my lungs were so damaged by my previous bouts with pneumonia that they were on the verge of collapse.

During that hospital stay, something really different happened. Eileen stopped by to visit with me. Eileen came in, sat right next to me on the bed, and asked me if she could have items from my meal tray. I was so shocked at her behavior and wondered to myself; "Does she know I have AIDS?" No one will ever know just how good it felt not to be treated like someone who had an contagious disease. I later asked Eileen about that and she said, "I trust God to protect me, so I don't need to think about things like that."

While the doctors put me through treatments to prevent pneumonia, they came out with a new combination of drugs called a cocktail that was having some success with AIDS patients. They explained I would be taking thirty-three pills a day, and in the first month I could expect the medication to make me very ill. I couldn't wait! *Right!* I was in tears as they were explaining the process to me. I never was a good pill taker.

The first day on the medication, I was crying because the pills were hard to get down and I was becoming sick before I took them all. I called Eileen in tears as I told her how horrible the experience was for me. She said my nerves were probably getting in the way and she would come over to help me. Every day she faithfully came over to make sure I kept the pills down and stayed calm. I can truly say that if she had not been so diligent, I would have stopped taking the pills because of what they were doing to me. The side effects, though, started to diminish after about two weeks on the medication.

After a couple of months, my results started to improve. My doctor said he never expected to see the kind of improvement I was experiencing, and frankly he was surprised I was still alive.

In July 1997, I was in the hospital again—this time for a hysterectomy because my PAP smears never improved. Blessedly my AIDS symptoms improved, because they would not have scheduled me for surgery with the low blood counts I had had just five months before. Eileen and my mother were with me when I went into surgery. The procedure was to take about forty-five minutes to an hour. Eileen told me later that my mother was planning my funeral because I was in the operating room for over three hours, and she was sure the news was bad. The procedure was more complicated than the doctors expected, but all went well. After one setback that caused me to be readmitted, a couple of months were needed for me to recover from the surgery.

In the fall of 1997, my medication was no longer working so I started another cocktail. This change became a pattern because, after six months or so, my system would build up resistance to the drugs I was taking. This resistance caused the doctors some frustration; at one point, the doctor told me I had been on every combination available at the time. Little did he know that God was giving more insight to researchers and new drugs were in the pipeline.

On September 30, 1998, I celebrated my fortieth birthday! I was told I would never see this day. I own a cemetery plot I purchased to keep my family from being burdened financially as a result of my death. The year 1998 would turn out to be the first year since my diagnosis when I did not spend any time in the hospital.

It's now 2003. I'm down from thirty-three pills a day to sixteen. I weigh 120 pounds, and my doctor is amazed every time I show up for an appointment. I've attended so many funerals for people diagnosed later than me, and for some who weren't even sick. Eileen reminds me of how far I've come when I voice my frustrations with my physical limitations and the never-end-ing routine with my medications. I only want to be more active because I know God has given me this time to do work for Him, and my lack of stamina limits how much I can do in His service.

In spite of my limitations, I have served as the volunteer secretary in the church office, I conduct twelfth-grade vacation Bible school class, I cochair the young women's mentoring network, and I direct the sanctuary choir. God is so good.

I feel I have grown tremendously at Colonial, which is truly a Bible teaching church. The members are constantly lifting me up in prayer and giving support whenever I need it. I have seen how God used the tough times in my life to prepare me for something great. Now my life is no longer about living or dying; it's about seeing the power of God. The fact that I can tell this story is such a blessing. To God be the glory, and it's all because of Christ's love for me.

I don't know if I will live to see this book published; tomorrow is not promised to me. I know if one person gains some insight, help, or encouragement from what I have shared, this book will not have been written in vain. If I am not around when this book is published, please tell whoever you share it with that no matter what the trial or tragedy, "God meant it for good."

To order additional copies of

GOD MEANT IT *for* GOOD

The Alice T. Brown Story

Have your credit card ready and call:

1-877-421-READ (7323)

or please visit our web site at
www.pleasantword.com

Also available at: www.amazon.com

Printed in the United States
1295600001B/191